First World War
and Army of Occupation
War Diary
France, Belgium and Germany

59 DIVISION
178 Infantry Brigade
Sherwood Foresters
(Nottinghamshire and Derbyshire Regiment)
2/8th Battalion
1 November 1914 - 29 October 1916

WO95/3025/7

The Naval & Military Press Ltd
www.nmarchive.com
Published in association with The National Archives

Published by

The Naval & Military Press Ltd

Unit 10 Ridgewood Industrial Park,

Uckfield, East Sussex,

TN22 5QE England

Tel: +44 (0) 1825 749494

www.naval-military-press.com

www.nmarchive.com

This diary has been reprinted in facsimile from the original. Any imperfections are inevitably reproduced and the quality may fall short of modern type and cartographic standards.

© **Crown Copyright**
Images reproduced by permission of The National Archives, London, England, 2015.

Contents

Document type	Place/Title	Date From	Date To
Heading	WO 3025 59 Div 178 Br 2/8 Bn Sherwood Foresters 1914 Nov-1916 Feb		
Heading	59 Division 178 Brigade 2/8 Bn Sherwood Foresters 1914 Nov-1916 Feb		
Heading	War Diaries Of 2/8th Sherwood Foresters November & December 1914		
War Diary	Newark.	01/11/1914	30/11/1914
Miscellaneous	2/8th Battalion The Sherwood Foresters.		
War Diary	Newark	01/12/1914	23/12/1914
Miscellaneous	December 1914		
Heading	War Diaries Of 2/8th Sherwood Foresters January To December 1915.		
Miscellaneous	Salonica Army War Diary.		
Miscellaneous	Cover For Documents. Nature Of Enclosures.		
War Diary	Rewards	01/01/1915	31/01/1915
Miscellaneous	2/8th Battalion The Sherwood Foresters.		
War Diary	Luton	01/02/1915	28/02/1915
Miscellaneous	2/8th Battn. The Sherwood Foresters		
War Diary	Luton	01/03/1915	31/03/1915
Miscellaneous	March 1915		
War Diary	Luton	01/04/1915	30/04/1915
Miscellaneous	April, 1915		
War Diary	Luton	01/05/1915	31/05/1915
Miscellaneous	2/8th Battn. The Sherwood Foresters		
War Diary	Luton	01/06/1915	07/06/1915
War Diary	Dunstable	27/06/1915	30/06/1915
Miscellaneous	2/8th Battn. The Sherwood Foresters		
War Diary	Dunstable	01/07/1915	31/07/1915
Miscellaneous	Statement To Accompany War Diary For The Month Of July 1915.		
War Diary	Dunstable	01/08/1915	11/08/1915
War Diary	Watford	31/08/1915	31/08/1915
Miscellaneous	Statement To Accompany War Diary For The Month Of August 1915.		
War Diary	Watford	01/09/1915	30/09/1915
Miscellaneous	Statement To Company War Diary September 1916	04/12/1915	04/12/1915
War Diary	Watford	01/10/1915	31/10/1915
Miscellaneous	2/8 Boa Sherwood Foresters October 1915		
War Diary	Watford	01/11/1915	30/11/1915
Miscellaneous	November 1915	06/12/1915	06/12/1915
War Diary	Watford	01/12/1915	31/12/1915
Miscellaneous	2/8th Battalion The Sherwood Foresters.		
Heading	War Diary Of 2/8th Bn Sherwood Foresters From 1st To 31st January 1916 Volume 16		
War Diary	Watford	01/01/1916	31/01/1916
Miscellaneous	January 1916	02/02/1916	02/02/1916
Heading	War Diary Of 2/8 Battalion Sherwood Foresters War Diary For The Month Of February 1916 Volume Xvi		
War Diary	Watford	01/10/1916	29/10/1916

Miscellaneous | Appendix. To Accompany Volume 16 War Diary Of February 1916. | 29/02/1916 29/02/1916

WO 3025
59 Div 178Br
2/8 BN Sherwood Foresters
1914 Nov — 1916 Feb

59 DIVISION

178 BRIGADE

2/8 BN SHERWOOD FORESTERS

1914 NOV — 1916 FEB

War diaries of
2/8th Sherwood Foresters.

November & December
1914.

2/8th Battn. Sherwood Foresters.
WAR DIARY
or
INTELLIGENCE SUMMARY.
(Erase heading not required.)

Army Form C. 2118.

Instructions regarding War Diaries and Intelligence
Summaries are contained in F. S. Regs, Part II.
and the Staff Manual respectively. Title pages
will be prepared in manuscript.

Place	Date	Hour	Summary of Events and Information	Remarks and references to Appendices
Newark.	1914 Nov. 1st		This Battalion came into existence. Strength Rank & File 539.	
"	2nd.	6-30.a.m to 7-30.a.m	Bathing Parade & Physical Drill	
"		9.a.m. to 12-30.p.m	Company Training on The Grove, Balderton.	
"		2.p.m. to 4.p.m.	Battalion Drill on The Grove, Balderton.	
			The above is given as an example of the work done during the month of November by the Battn.	
"	7th		2nd Lieut. Alfred Hacking and 100 men were transferred to the 8th Battalion Sherwood Foresters then stationed at Harpenden to form the 1st Reinforcements.	
"	14th		2nd Lieut. F.B.Hemmingway and 22 men were transferred to the 8th Battalion as above to fill up vacancies.	
"	30th		Strength Rank & File 765.	

W. [signature] Lieut-Colonel.
Commanding 2/8th Battn. THE SHERWOOD FORESTERS.

2/8th Battalion THE SHERWOOD FORESTERS.

Appendix to War Diary November 1914.

This Battalion consisted of Officers, N.C.O's and Men who were transferred from the 8th Battalion Sherwood Foresters for one of the following reasons:-

(1) Training the new Battalion

(2) Medically Unfit

(3) Unwilling to undertake the Imperial Service Obligation.

In addition to Officers and men who joined for the Austro-German War which was commenced in August 1914.

Practically all the men who were transferred from the 1st 8th Battalion were on detachment during the month of November and were engaged on fatigue work at Dunstable where they helped to construct a Field Firing Range. The remainder of the Battalion was quartered at Newark-on-Trent.

This was a good arrangement as it enabled the Officers to get good hold of the men who joined for the War and to train them away from the men transferred from the 1st 8th who were naturally not the best specimens of their Battalion.

The men were accomodated in private billets and in their own homes at the 3/9 rate an extravagant arrangement in a place like Newark where the people would gladly have taken the soldiers in at 2/6 or even less.

The effect on discipline of billets is never good but the men were keen and there was no serious crime.

The Notts Territorial Force Association clothed the men with wonderful despatch and after the first two weeks there was ample clothing and necessaries for all.

With regard to Recruiting I am of opinion that a serious mistake was made in allowing any men to enlist for home defence in this Battalion at that time practically the same number would have been obtained if the Imperial Service obligation had been made compulsory but a still more serious mistake was made in stopping recruiting from time to time. When a man has once been refused experience shows that he is very difficult to catch a second time and a great many men had to be refused to comply with Regulations during the month of December.

A better plan would have been to have formed two Battalions one for Home Defence consisting of Married Men and those who could not or would

(2)

not undertake Imperial Service and a second for Imperial Service men only.

A considerable number of men were cast for height and chest measurement.

Civilian Practitioners were on the whole very careful in the men they passed.

Recruiting for the Territorial Force was done in conjunction with recruiting for the Army and later on many men who wished to join the Territorial Force were sent to the Army at times when our recruiting was stopped.

The work of organising a new Battalion kept Officers and men, most of whom had but limited experience of military matters, hard at work so that no time could be spared to organise a Recruiting March or indeed to visit other parts of the County but every endeavour was made in the neighbourhood of Newark to get Recruits and on route marches the Battalion was timed to pass the principal Works in the Town as the Employees left their work. This plan proved efficacious as undoubtedly the Bugle Band which was of excellent merit helped to attract Recruits and the men themselves did not hesitate to impress on likely recruits their feeling that they should join.

Men did not suffer from lack of proper sanitation.

W Cope Oates   Lieut-Colonel
Commanding 2/8th Sherwood Foresters.

Army Form C. 2118.

WAR DIARY
or
INTELLIGENCE SUMMARY.
(Erase heading not required.)

Instructions regarding War Diaries and Intelligence Summaries are contained in F. S. Regs., Part II. and the Staff Manual respectively. Title pages will be prepared in manuscript.

Place	Date	Hour	Summary of Events and Information	Remarks and references to Appendices
Newark	1914 Jan. 1st	—	Strength. Figures not available	
"	31st	—	—do— —do—	
"	23rd	—	A Draft of 25 Men proceeded to Braintree to fill vacancies in the 1st Line	

Watford,
6th Decr. 1915.

W. Trafford,
Lt-Colonel,
Commanding
2/8th Bn. Sherwood Foresters.

T.1134. Wt. W708—776. 500000. 4/15. Sir J. C. & S.

DECEMBER 1914

The same attention was paid during this month to Squad, Company and Battalion Drill which was, however, varied on one or two occasions by an Outpost Day. The Men were keen on this and soon picked up their duties.

They had also an opportunity, for the first time, of using rifles, the system adopted was for the young Officers and N.C.O's to be first instructed by a senior Officer with a view to their afterwards instructing their men. This plan was very successful.

Unfortunately the figures with regard to strength are not available for this month as these records have not been preserved.

A proper strength book was begun on February 1st 1915.

H Coape Oates Lt-Colonel,
Commanding,
2/8th Battn. THE SHERWOOD FORESTERS.

WATFORD,
6th December 1915.

War Diaries of
2/8th Sherwood Foresters.

January to December
1915.

Volume No. 5 1 to 4

SALONICA ARMY

WAR DIARY.

Unit 20th Heavy Battery R.G.A. — 39th Heavy Arty Group A.S.

Vol. No.	From		To	
1.	12th October 1916	To	31st October 1916
2.	1st November 1916	to	30th November 1916
3.	1st December 1916	to	31st December 1916
4.	1st January 1917	to	31st January 1917

Army Form W. 3091.

Cover for Documents.

Nature of Enclosures.

143 Inf Bde
misc files
Nov 1916

Notes, or Letters written.

Culford

Army Form C. 2118.

WAR DIARY
or
INTELLIGENCE SUMMARY.
(Erase heading not required.)

Instructions regarding War Diaries and Intelligence Summaries are contained in F. S. Regs., Part II. and the Staff Manual respectively. Title pages will be prepared in manuscript.

Place	Date	Hour	Summary of Events and Information	Remarks and references to Appendices
Newark	1915 May 1st		Strength Figures not available	
"	" 2nd		Inspection by Lieut-Gen. Sir Reginald Pole Carew, K.C.B., C.V.O.	
"	" 31st		Strength Figures not available	

Watford.

M. Rapt Dale.
Lieut-Colonel.
Commanding, 2/8th Sherwood Foresters.

T2134. Wt. W708—776. 500000. 4/15. Sir J. C. & S.

Confidential

2/8th Battalion THE SHERWOOD FORESTERS.

On January 2nd 1915, The Battalion was inspected by Lieut.Gen. The Hon. Sir. Reginald Pole Carew, K.C.B., C.V.O., at Newark.

The Battalion received the Inspecting General with the General Present. Salute

The Inspecting General at the conclusion of the Inspection expressed himself as not only pleased, but amazed at the results which had been arrived at in so short a time, and congratulated all Ranks in their steadiness.

This was accomplished by the keenness of the men and from the fact that and Officers and N.C.O's from the very beginning impressed on all Ranks the necessity of steadiness in the Ranks as the first thing a Soldier had to do.

Commanding, W. Capoate   Lieut-Colonel.
2/8th Battn. Sherwood Foresters.

WATFORD.

2/8 Batt.
Sherwood Foresters

1915.   168 N.C.Os & Men
Nov.10.   1 Transferred to
              29th Provisional Batt

           23 to 3/8.
   16.   6
            5. Discharged
            2. Struck off
               1868. K.R.
               (Deserters)
            1. Discharged
   17.   5. to 29 Prov. Batt
            1. to 2/7. Notts &
                        Derby
   22.   2 Discharged
            3   Do
   25.   1.   Do
   28.   1. to 3/8 Batt.
   29.   1. to 29 Prov.
   30.   2. to 29 Batt.
            ―――
            114
            ═══

           A.B.R. [signature]
           Capt. & Adjt.

Confidential

WAR DIARY
or
INTELLIGENCE SUMMARY.

(Erase heading not required.)

Army Form C. 2118.

2/8 Batt. Sherwood Foresters

Place	Date	Hour	Summary of Events and Information	Remarks and references to Appendices
Luton	1915 Feby 1st		Strength, 25 Officers, 1032 Other Ranks.	n/a
"	"		Battalion removed from Newark to Luton	n/a
"	" 8th		Battalion removed from Luton to Billericay	n/a
"	" 22nd		85 N.C.O's & Men transferred to 1/8th Battalion at Braintree	n/a
"	"		3 Officers transferred to 1/8th Battalion at Braintree	n/a
"	" 23rd		85 N.C.O's & Men transferred from 1/8th Battalion at Braintree	n/a
"	" 24th		Battalion removed from Billericay to Luton	n/a
"	" 28th		Strength, Officers 22, Other Ranks 1043. The increase of Other Ranks is accounted for by 5 R.A.M.C. Men being attached and 6 Men being transferred from Depot.	n/a

Hape Oates Lt. Col.
Commanding
2/8th Bn. Sherwood Foresters

Confidential

Statement to accompany [...] for February 1915

2/8th Battn. THE SHERWOOD FORESTERS

1915.
Feby. 1st.   The Battalion left Newark and proceeded to Luton, there to take its place in the 2/1st Notts. & Derby Brigade of which Col. W. Wright Hemrose V.D. was in Command. The Brigade was part of the 2/1st North Midland Division, Commanded by Brigadier General H.B. McCall C.B.

Government Rations were issued for the first time. Considerable difficulty was found in the first few days at Luton owing to the fact that there were no proper appliances for chopping up and issuing meat and other rations.

Feby. 5th   The name of the Battalion was altered from the 8th (Res) Battn. Notts. & Derby to the 2/8th Notts. & Derby Battn., an alteration welcomed by all Ranks.

Feby. 8th   The Battalion left Luton and proceeded to Billericay in Essex for the purpose of being instructed in Entrenching. Here they were joined by the Members of the Battalion who had been on Detachment at North Weald.

Feby. 24th   The Battalion returned to Luton from Billericay.

Feby. 28th   Japanese Rifles were received and issued for the Battalion.

                         A. Coape Oates   Lieut-Colonel,
                Commanding,
                  2/8th Battn. THE SHERWOOD FORESTERS.

Luton February 1915

Army Form C. 2118.

WAR DIARY
or
INTELLIGENCE SUMMARY.
(Erase heading not required.)

2/8 B⁰ Sherwood Foresters

Instructions regarding War Diaries and Intelligence Summaries are contained in F. S. Regs., Part II. and the Staff Manual respectively. Title pages will be prepared in manuscript.

Place	Date	Hour	Summary of Events and Information	Remarks and references to Appendices
Luton	1915 March 1st		Strength, Officers 22. Other Ranks 1043.	H⁰
"	2nd		Battalion inspected by Sir Ian Hamilton, G.C.B., G.S.O., A.D.C., G. Oc-in-Chief, Central Force in Stockwood Park.	H⁰
"	3rd		Battalion inspected by Brigadier General H.B. McCall, C.B., Commanding, 2/1st (North Midland) Division in Stockwood Park.	H⁰
"	4th		Japanese Musketry Course commenced.	H⁰
"	31st		Strength, Officers 23. Other Ranks 1033. The difference of 10 is accounted for by 8 Men being transferred from Depot, 8 Men being transferred from 1/8th Battalion, 1 N.C.O. 1 Men being discharged, 1 Death, 18 N.C.Os transferred to Base Details.	H⁰

Hopedale Lt-Col.
Commanding,
2/8ᵗʰ Bn. Sherwood Foresters

[signature] 1st Feb 1916

Confidential

2/8 Bⁿ
Sherwood
Foresters

Statement to
accompany War Diary

MARCH 1915

- - - - - -

During this month an Active Service Company was formed
consisting of men medically fit who had undertaken the
Imperial Service obligation being transferred from other
Companies.   This system worked fairly well, though
it proved as events turned out that it would have been better
to have continued the old system of having an Active Service
Platoon in each Company for the reason that when a large
Draft was called for it left this particular Company
Completely denuded of men of any Standing thereby making
their Training all the more difficult.

          W Coape Oates   Lieut-Colonel,
   Commanding,
     2/8th Battn. THE SHERWOOD FORESTERS.

Luton, March 1915.
~~WATFORD~~,
~~1st February 1916.~~

WAR DIARY
or
INTELLIGENCE SUMMARY.
(Erase heading not required.)

Army Form C. 2118.

2/8 B... Sherwood Foresters

Place	Date	Hour	Summary of Events and Information	Remarks and references to Appendices
Luton	1915 April 1st	12h.	Strength, Officers 24, Other Ranks 1033.	H.Q.
"			A very interesting Concentration March took place. This Battalion arriving at the Concentration Point within 10 seconds of the allotted time. The calculation was based on 3 miles an hour.	H.Q.
"		3 O.R.	Strength, Officers 24, Other Ranks 1063. The difference is accounted for by 31 Men being transferred from Depot & 1 Man being discharged.	H.Q.

Karl Oates Lt-Col.
Commanding
2/8th Bn. Sherwood Foresters.

Confidential Statements accompany War Diary 2/8 Battn. Sherwood Foresters

APRIL, 1915

There is nothing of much note to be recorded this month.
Training was continued and Musketry carried on.
During the month Horses were issued to the Battalion.
They were a sorry lot when first received but with care,
regular feeding and exercise, quickly improved and
developed in a few weeks time to a really useful lot.

                         [signature] Lieut-Colonel,
      Commanding.
      2/8th Battn. THE SHERWOOD FORESTERS.

~~KARRAKA,~~
   ~~1st February 1916.~~

Luln 1915

Confidential

2/8 Batt
Sherwood Foresters

WAR DIARY
or
INTELLIGENCE SUMMARY.
(Erase heading not required.)

Army Form C. 2118.

Instructions regarding War Diaries and Intelligence Summaries are contained in F.S. Regs., Part II. and the Staff Manual respectively. Title pages will be prepared in manuscript.

Place	Date	Hour	Summary of Events and Information	Remarks and references to Appendices
Retford	1915		Strength 1070.	Rolls
	Mar 4		5 Officers and 175 Other Ranks proceeded to Retford on a Recruiting March and returned on Mar 11.	Rolls
	31		Posted 28 [Others] Recruits. Strength 1235.	Rolls

Makdale
Lt. Col.
Commanding
2/8 Bn Sherwood Foresters

CONFIDENTIAL

2/8th Battn. THE SHERWOOD FORESTERS

STATEMENT TO ACCOMPANY WAR DIARY FOR THE MONTH OF MAY 1915.

During this month a special appeal was made by the Colonel for men who had enlisted for Home Defence to take on the Imperial Service obligation in view of the fact that hopes were held out that this Battalion might proceed Overseas as a Unit. There was a fine response to this appeal, nearly 250 N.C.O's and Men undertaking the Imperial Service obligation.

The Recruiting March which took place during this month had successful results, due largely to the facts that by means of being accompanied by the Medical Officer and Clothing it was possible to enlist the men on the spot and the newly joined Recruits to accompany the Detachment on the remainder of the March.
Everywhere the Detachment was received with the greatest kindness and hospitality by the inhabitants.

[signature]   Lieut-Colonel,
Commanding,
2/8th Battn. THE SHERWOOD FORESTERS.

~~WATFORD,~~
~~March 1916.~~

CONFIDENTIAL

Confidential   2/8 Batt. Sherwood Foresters

WAR DIARY
or
INTELLIGENCE SUMMARY.
(Erase heading not required.)

Army Form C. 2118.

Instructions regarding War Diaries and Intelligence Summaries are contained in F. S. Regs., Part II. and the Staff Manual respectively. Title pages will be prepared in manuscript.

Place	Date	Hour	Summary of Events and Information	Remarks and references to Appendices
Luton	1915 June 1		Strength 1235 The Battalion consisting of Imperial Service Men only proceeded from Luton to Dunstable Camp.	H.O.
"	" 7		The Home Defence Men remaining in Luton, the number of these was Officers 2, Other Ranks 138.	H.O.
Dunstable	" 27	.30	A Draft of 361 N.C.O's & Men were transferred to British Expeditionary Force. Strength 719.	H.O.

Moorsdale Lt- Col.
Commanding
2/8th Sherwood Foresters

CONFIDENTIAL

2/8th Battn. THE SHERWOOD FORESTERS

STATEMENT TO ACCOMPANY WAR DIARY FOR THE MONTH OF JUNE 1915.

During this month the men who enlisted for Home Defence were transferred to a Provisional Battalion and on the 6th June the following notice appeared in Battalion Orders :-

"On the Battalion leaving its present quarters the
"Commanding Officer wishes to express his congratulations
"and thanks to all ranks for their continued good
"behaviour and the progress they have made in their
"training during the time the Regiment has been stationed
"at Luton. In parting with the members of the
"Battalion who are about to join the Provisional Home
"Defence Battalion, which he does with regret, he wishes
"to call their attention to the fact that the reputation
"of both the 1/8th and 2/8th Battalions lies to some
"extent in their hands and he relies on them that at no
"time will they allow the good name of those who are
"undertaking the Imperial Service obligation to suffer at
"their hands".

On the 27th of this month a draft of 361 N.C.O's and Men proceeded overseas to join the British Expeditionary Force. The following was inserted in Battalion Orders on 27th June 1915 :-

"On this large Draft proceeding to join the British Expedition-
"ary Force the Commanding Officer wishes to express his
"good wishes to all ranks who are proceeding and to place
"on record his appreciation of the Good Conduct, Efficiency
"and Discipline which the men have displayed in the past.
"He wishes to remind them that on Active Service Discipline
"is of necessity stricter than at Home Stations but he is
"confident that he can absolutely rely on every man
"whereever his Duty may call him to be a credit to this
"Battalion and to the 1/8th Battalion who have already
"rendered so splendid an account of themselves in the Trenches".

                                              [signature]   Lieut-Colonel,
                                Commanding,
                      2/8th Battn. THE SHERWOOD FORESTERS.

~~WATFORD~~,
  ~~March 1916~~.

Confidential

2/8th Batt
Sherwood Foresters

WAR DIARY
or
INTELLIGENCE SUMMARY.
(Erase heading not required.)

Army Form C. 2118.

Instructions regarding War Diaries and Intelligence Summaries are contained in F. S. Regs., Part II. and the Staff Manual respectively. Title pages will be prepared in manuscript.

Place	Date	Hour	Summary of Events and Information	Remarks and references to Appendices
Dunstable	1915 July 1		Strength 719	H.O.
	14		181 Men were transferred from the 3/8th Battalion at Newark-on-Trent to this Battalion	H.O.
	19		Resignation of Col. W. Wright Penrose V.D.	H.O.
			Command of the Brigade taken over by Col. E. W. S. K. Maconchy C.B., C.I.E., D.S.O.	H.O.
	31		Strength 860.	H.O.

W.Y. Oake Lt-Col.
Commanding
2/8th Sherwood Foresters.

CONFIDENTIAL

2/8th Battn. THE SHERWOOD FORESTERS

STATEMENT TO ACCOMPANY WAR DIARY FOR THE MONTH
OF JULY 1915.

During the month of July the usual training took place and there is really nothing of any note to record. except that Col. E. W. S. Maconchy, C.B. C.I.E. D.S.O took command of the Brigade.

W Toape Oates Lieut-Colonel,
Commanding,
2/8th Battn. THE SHERWOOD FORESTERS.

~~WATFORD~~,
~~March 1916~~.

2/8¢ Batt.
Sherwood Foresters.

Confidential

WAR DIARY
or
INTELLIGENCE SUMMARY.

(Erase heading not required.)

Army Form C. 2118.

Instructions regarding War Diaries and Intelligence Summaries are contained in F. S. Regs., Part II. and the Staff Manual respectively. Title pages will be prepared in manuscript.

Place	Date	Hour	Summary of Events and Information	Remarks and references to Appendices
Dunstable	1915 Aug 1		Strength. 860.	H.O.
"	"		Battalion removed from Dunstable Camp to Watford Camp by Road.	H.O.
Watford	31		Strength. 779.	H.O.

Hope Oates
Lt Col.
Commanding
2/8th Sherwood Foresters.

CONFIDENTIAL

2/8th Battn. THE SHERWOOD FORESTERS

STATEMENT TO ACCOMPANY WAR DIARY FOR THE MONTH
OF AUGUST 1915.

On the 15th August, 80 N.C.O's and Men proceeded Overseas to join the British Expeditionary Force.

Special attention was paid to Digging during this month.

There is nothing of very great importance to record this month.

                                                      H. Coape Oates   Lieut-Colonel,

                                                          Commanding,
                                                  2/8th Battn. THE SHERWOOD FORESTERS.

~~WATFORD~~,

~~March 1916~~.

Confidential

2/8. Sher. F.

Army Form C. 2118.

WAR DIARY
or
INTELLIGENCE SUMMARY.
(Erase heading not required.)

Instructions regarding War Diaries and Intelligence Summaries are contained in F. S. Regs., Part II. and the Staff Manual respectively. Title pages will be prepared in manuscript.

Place	Date	Hour	Summary of Events and Information	Remarks and references to Appendices
Watford	1915 Sept 1st		Strength. Officers 28. Rank & File 779.	H.Q.1
"	" 15th	11-0 a.m. to 1-30 p.m.	Inspection by the G.O.C. 59" (North Midland) Division in Gorhambury Park, St. Albans.	H.Q.
"	" 30th		Strength. Officers 27. Rank & File 771.	H.Q.

Watford,
14th December 1915.

Major Oates Lt-Colonel
Commanding 2/8th Bn. Sherwood Foresters.

Statement to accompany War Diary
September 1916

Confidential

2/8th Battn. THE SHERWOOD FORESTERS.

During the month of September the Battalion for the first time took part in Brigade and Divisional Operations.

This was of advantage as it provided a break in the usual routine which cannot, despite every endeavour, be made interesting to the men.

The men showed keenness and interest in the work more especially in outpost work where a certain amount of individuality is needed.

A great deal of Digging was done during this month, for which the men showed special aptitude.

Night Operations were also carried out and lines of Trenches sited by Officers Commanding Companies.

The Transport had the opportunity of learning how to load horses and wagons on Rail in connection with the Emergency Move early in the Month.

The Battalion was also inspected by the Brigadier General at Gorhambury Park with the rest of the Division.
It was a splendid site for such an Inspection and the Troops presented a fine appearance.

An Inspection such as this is of the greatest use as it helps more than anything else to produce a feeling among all Ranks of the great Esprit de Corps of a Brigade or a Division as compared with that of a Battalion or Company. The men were just as keen that the 178th Infantry Brigade should compare well with the other Brigades of the Division and that the Division should do well as a whole as that their own Battalion or Company should deserve merit and I think it made them realise that they were a part of a great organization and that on their individual efforts the credit of all concerned rested.

The enormous work of Dental Treatment continued this Month. I consider that one of the most important things for the Civil Authorities is to devise some scheme by which greater inducement should be held out to Parents to see that their Childrens Teeth are attended to properly in their youth and Neglect of Teeth should be made an offence punishable by law.
If Drastic Measures are not taken in this matter from the experience I have gained I am convinced that the future of the Civil Population, let alone the British Army, will in years to come be most seriously

2/8th Battn. THE SHERWOOD FORESTERS

2

(continued)

impaired.

M Hoape Oates Lt Colonel
Officer Commanding,
2/8th Battn. THE SHERWOOD FORESTERS.

WATFORD,
4th December 1915.

Colonels

2/8 Batt Sherwood Foresters

Army Form C. 2118.

WAR DIARY
or
INTELLIGENCE SUMMARY.
(Erase heading not required.)

Place	Date	Hour	Summary of Events and Information	Remarks and references to Appendices
Watford	1915 Oct 1	11.45 a.m.	The Battalion was inspected by General Sir Leslie Rundle G.C.B. G.C.V.O. D.S.O. at Johnson Park St Albans with the rest of the Brigade	
			General R. O. 30 Officers including 2/O 11 Officers transferred to 769 Siege Park	see appendix
	6		Complimentary Notice appeared in Battalion Orders	
	18		Battalion received anti-Bivets	
	31		General R. 27 the Officers including 2 O 10 Officers struck off establishment 767 & 770 Ends	

L.W.B. Wright Maj.
Officer Commanding
the O.C. 7th Sherwood Foresters

Oct. 19.15 2/8 Batt. Sherwood Foresters.
Copy of Complimentary Notice

The G.O.C. has much pleasure in publishing
the following letter from the G.O.C. in C.
Central Force, on his Inspection on
Friday last.

I am directed by G.O.C. in C. to inform
you that he was greatly impressed by the
appearance of the Division under your
Command at his Inspection on Friday last.
The Bearing of all Ranks and their
Steadiness on Parade were excellent.
He was also pleased to note the
good turn out and the efficient manner
any movements ordered were carried out.

The C. in C. is fully aware of the
many difficulties the Divisional Commander
and those under him have had to
contend with, which only goes to shew
that all Ranks have made the most
of their opportunities & have produced
the satisfactory results he saw.

L. C. B. Appleby Major
for & in the absence of
the O.C. 2/8 Sherwood Foresters

2/8th Battn.
Sherwood Foresters.

October 1915

During this month the Battalion moved from Camp which they had occupied since June into Billets.

The System of Billeting is unfortunate though obviously unavoidable.

It is impossible to maintain the same supervision in Billets as in Camp, and the difficulties both as to Discipline and Organization are greatly increased.

For the first time this Battalion has been fed centrally, & this System has worked well.

Some of the men after a period were moved from Billets into Central Sleeping Halls.

This was rather unfortunate. The men felt the comparative discomfort of Central Sleeping after the luxury of Billets much more than they would have done if ever they had gone into the Halls straight from the Camp.

Further it would seem better that, if possible, the same arrangement for all was in vogue.

Those men who are sleeping centrally have taken it in a soldier like spirit but they are clearly not so comfortable as their fellows.

The same difficulty with regard to drying wet clothes as existed in Camp remains for these men

L.C.P. Appleby Major

for in the absence of
the OC 2/8 Sherwood Foresters

2/8 Batt. Sherwood Foresters
October 1915

The new System of reduction of
meat for tea, here was begun
this month.

The effect is not satisfactory
as it is impossible to give the
men more than Bread and Jam
for their Teas.

This meant that tea & no chiefly
solid food between 1. P.M. and
7. a.m. the next morning

L.W. Appleby Major
from the absence of
the O.C. Sherwood Foresters

Army Form C. 2118.

WAR DIARY
or
INTELLIGENCE SUMMARY.
(Erase heading not required.)

Instructions regarding War Diaries and Intelligence Summaries are contained in F. S. Regs., Part II. and the Staff Manual respectively. Title pages will be prepared in manuscript.

Place	Date	Hour	Summary of Events and Information	Remarks and references to Appendices
Watford	1915 Nov 1st	—	Strength, Rank & File 767.	
"		11-30am	Battalion inspected by Major General G.T. Bickram Inspector General of Infantry on Cattermland	
"		10-30pm	Battalion inspected by Major General R.N.R. Reade, C.B. Commanding 59th (North Midland) Division.	
"	29R	—	Company Training commenced	
"	30R	—	Strength, Rank & File 653.	

Watford,
6th Decr. 1915.

Mabe Oak, Lt-Colonel,
Commanding,
2/8th Bn. Sherwood Foresters.

NOVEMBER 1915

There is nothing of real note to chronicle during this month except that two Inspections took place, one by the Inspector General of Infantry and the other by our new Divisional Commander, Major General R.N.R.Reade C.B. who had succeeded Brigadier General H.B.McCall C.B. in Command of the 59th (North Midland) Division. During the latter days of the month orders were received that our establishment of Officers was to be reduced to 23.

The result of this was the loss of some valuable and promising young Officers who joined the 3rd Line.

On the other Hand the order stated that no more Officers would be taken from us to join the 1st Line so that on the whole the arrangement was for the benefit of the 2nd Line, however much the However, the loss of these Officers may have been regretted at the time.

In this connection it may be of interest to note that since November 1st 1914 no less than 63 Officers, including attached, have been with this Battalion, 23 having proceeded Overseas.

                                          W.Crape Oates Lieut-Colonel,
Commanding,
2/8th Battn. THE SHERWOOD FORESTERS.

WATFORD,
6th December 1915.

Confidential

Army Form C. 2118.

WAR DIARY
or
INTELLIGENCE SUMMARY.
(Erase heading not required.)

Instructions regarding War Diaries and Intelligence Summaries are contained in F.S. Regs., Part II. and the Staff Manual respectively. Title pages will be prepared in manuscript.

Place	Date	Hour	Summary of Events and Information	Remarks and references to Appendices
Watford	1915 Dec 1st		Strength Officers 23, R.S attached 1, attached for Instruction 5, R&F of file 653	
"	" 31st		" " 23, " " 1, " " 5, " " 644	

Watford

Maple Oaks Lieut-Colonel
Commanding 2/8th Sherwood Foresters

2/8th Battalion THE SHERWOOD FORESTERS.

During the month of December 1915, 2 Companies, "C" & "D"., were struck off all Duties and went through a Course of Company Training.   Unforthuately they were very much handicapped by the weather during the whole time.   The result was, however, wholly beneficial and the gain in efficiency was very satisfactory.

An exercise in Administrative Duties took place which was of most absorbing interest and extremely instructive.

The question of saving Bye Products was carefully studied this month.

It is a matter of great importance as it is recognised that the saving which can be effected when multiplied by the large a number of men under Arms at the present time can only be described as Colossal.

                                           W. Coape Oates   Lieut-Colonel.
                       Commanding,
W A T F O R D.   2/8th Battn. THE SHERWOOD FORESTERS.

Confidential

War Diary

of

7/8 Bn Sherwood Foresters

From 1st to 31st January 1916

Volume

Army Form C. 2118.

WAR DIARY
or
INTELLIGENCE SUMMARY.
(Erase heading not required.)

2/8 N. Sher. 2n

Instructions regarding War Diaries and Intelligence Summaries are contained in F.S. Regs., Part II. and the Staff Manual respectively. Title pages will be prepared in manuscript.

Place	Date	Hour	Summary of Events and Information	Remarks and references to Appendices
Watford	1916 Jan. 13th		Strength, Officers 23, Other Ranks 644	H.O.
"	17th		Capt. J.C. Martyn transferred to 3/8th Sherwood Foresters, Grantham.	H.O.
"	23rd		First party of "Derby Recruits" (32 men) arrived from Administrative Centre, Newark	H.O.
"	25th		25 Recruits transferred from Administrative Centre.	H.O.
"	27th		27 N.C.Os. & Men transferred to 29th Provisional Battalion, Wynberg.	H.O.
"	28th		31 Recruits transferred from Administrative Centre	M.O.
"	31st		33 Recruits transferred from Administrative Centre	H.O.
"	31st		Strength, Officers 22, Other Ranks 732.	H.O.
			The decrease in strength of Officers is accounted for by Capt. Martyn being transferred to the 3/8th Sherwood Foresters, Belton Park, Grantham.	
			Increase of strength in Other Ranks as follows:-	
			Discharge of 9 men, transfer of 27 N.C.Os. & Men to 29th Provisional Battalion, Wynberg.	
			3 Men transferred to the Battn. from 3/8th Sherwood Foresters, Grantham.	
			121 "Derby Recruits" transferred from Administrative Centre, Newark	H.O.

Watford,
2nd Feby. 1916

H/Cpl Oates
Lt-Col.
Commanding 2/8th Sherwood Foresters.

Confidential

JANUARY 1916

The Company Training of "A" & "B" Companies took place this month with first rate results. All Details going back to their Companies for this Special Training. This system of Company Training is altogether excellent. The men were hard worked but in spite of this did not get stale.

The first batch of Recruits enlisted under the Group System commonly known as "Derby Recruits" joined the Battalion this month. They were a likely lot and better still are recruited from a class hitherto hardly tapped namely Shop Assistants of whom there was a large percentage.

W. Coape Oates   Lieut-Colonel,

Commanding,
2/8th Battn. THE SHERWOOD FORESTERS.

WATFORD,
    2nd February 1916.

Confidential

2/8 Batt"
Sherwood Foresters

War Diary
for the
Month of
February 1916

Volume XVI

WAR DIARY or INTELLIGENCE SUMMARY

Army Form C. 2118.

2/8 Batt;
S. Stafford Regt.

Place	Date	Hour	Summary of Events and Information	Remarks and references to Appendices
Rugeley	1916 Dec 1		Strength Officers 22 (Others Ranks 721 attached 6)	RBT
	18		2 Officers and 100 Other Ranks proceeded to Swansea on Detachment Duty	RBT
	26		The Recruits were inspected by Major General A.E. Sandbach C.B. D.S.O. Commanding 59th (North Midland) Division	RBT
	28		Strength Officers 22 (Other Ranks 923 attached 6)	RBT
	29		The Difference in accounted for by 207 Recruits being taken on the Strength, 12 Men being discharged and 4 Men being transferred to other Corps.	RBT

Rugeley Dec 28th 1916.   Hugh Oak. Lt. Col.
Comdg 2/8 Bn S. Stafford Regt.

Confidential

2/8th Battn SHERWOOD FORESTERS.

A P P E N D I X. to accompany
Volume 16 War Dairy of February 1916.

The chief feature of this Month was the arrival of the remainder of the new Recruits. They were a well developed lot of Men, who speedily picked up their new duties and fell into line with other Men.

Their training has been carried out in accordance with the system adopted in the new Armies and when inspected by our new Divisional General they appeared to great advantage. This was a result of their being intelligent Men, great care being taken to select only the best Instructors, and by dint of Lectures to explain to them not only that they had to <u>do</u> certain things, but the <u>reason</u> why they had to do them.

The only regret is that this splendid material, available since the beginning of the War has only just been brought into line, when it might have been obtained and used from the first.

During this Month a detatchment of the Regiment proceeded to training Dunmow to act as a Guard to the G. O. C. 3rd Army. Company training was continued on modified lines, special attention being paid to the training of Bombers

W Coape Oates   Lt-Col,
                    Commanding 2/8th Sherwood Foresters.

WATFORD.
   29th Febry 1916.

www.ingramcontent.com/pod-product-compliance
Lightning Source LLC
Chambersburg PA
CBHW081457160426
43193CB00013B/2507